Tell Me Your Story, Grandmother

ILLUSTRATED BY Susan Wheeler

HARVEST HOUSE PUBLISHERS
EUGENE, OREGON

Tell Me Your Story, Grandmother

Artwork copyright © by Susan Wheeler
Text copyright © 2013 by Harvest House Publishers

Published by Harvest House Publishers
Eugene, Oregon 97402
www.harvesthousepublishers.com

ISBN 978-0-7369-5478-5

Susan Wheeler is represented by Alex Meisel & Co., LLC

Design and production by Garborg Design Works, Savage, Minnesota

Harvest House Publishers has made every effort to trace the ownership of all poems and quotes. In the event of a question arising from the use of a poem or quote, we regret any error made and will be pleased to make the necessary correction in future editions of this book.

All Scripture verses are taken from the Holy Bible, New Living Translation, copyright © 1996, 2004. Used by permission of Tyndale House Publishers, Inc., Wheaton, IL 60189 USA. All rights reserved.

Printed in China

13 14 15 16 17 18 19 20 /LP / 10 9 8 7 6 5 4 3 2 1

Tell me your story, Grandmother.

WITH LOVE,

_____

DATE

Just then thou didst recall to me
A distant long forgotten scene,
One smile, and one sweet word from thee
Dispelled the years that rolled between;
I was a little child again,
And every after joy and pain
Seemed never to have been.

ANNE BRONTË

It was Fritz who said it first, and when he was three years younger than
he is now. Somebody asked him what sort of stories he liked best. No doubt
he ought to have said "Bible Stories," such as his mother tells on Sunday
afternoons, and which he does love dearly. But he spoke out what he really
thought and felt at the time of asking, and said, "I like, best of all, to hear
about what happened when Grandmamma was New."

MARION HARLAND, FROM *WHEN GRANDMAMMA WAS NEW*

4

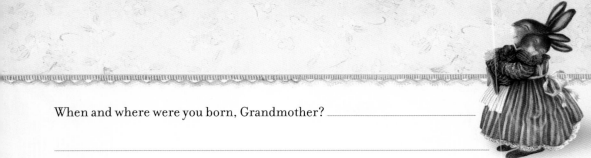

When and where were you born, Grandmother? _____

_____

Is there a story behind how you got your name? _____

_____

_____

Who were your parents? _____

Share a story you've been told about your birth or your early days of life. _____

_____

_____

_____

_____

_____

_____

_____

_____

_____

> *Heaven*
> *lies about*
> *us in our*
> *infancy.*
>
> WILLIAM
> WORDSWORTH

Family Story

A happy family is but
an earlier heaven.

SIR JOHN BOWRING

*Every child born
into the world is
a new incarnate
thought of God,
an ever-fresh
and radiant
possibility.*

KATE DOUGLAS WIGGIN

Where did your family originally come from? _____

_____

Who else was a part of your family? Siblings? Cousins? Aunts and uncles? _____

_____

_____

_____

Describe your parents and your home life. _____

_____

_____

_____

_____

Share a family story or memory that makes you smile. _____

_____

_____

_____

_____

_____

There is a magic in that little word, home; it is a mystic circle that
surrounds comforts and virtues never known beyond its hallowed limits.

ROBERT SOUTHEY

7

Girlhood

The heart hath its own memory, like the mind,
And in it are enshrined
The precious keepsakes, into which is wrought
The giver's loving thought.

HENRY WADSWORTH LONGFELLOW

What made you happiest when you were a girl? _____

_____

How did you spend a typical Saturday? _____

_____

_____

What were your favorite activities and hobbies? _____

_____

What was your prized possession as a girl? Why was it so important to you? ____

_____

_____

Share a story about your childhood. _____

_____

_____

_____

_____

_____

Youth is the gay and pleasant spring of life
When joy is stirring in the dancing blood,
And Nature calls us with a thousand songs,
To share her general feast.

JOSEPH RIDGEWAY

A Life of Learning

The interests
of childhood
and youth are
the interests of
mankind.

EDMUND STORER JANES

Children are not so much to be
taught as to be trained. To teach
a child is to give him ideas.

HENRY WARD BEECHER

Describe what your schools and classrooms were like when you were young. _____

_____

_____

_____

What school activities or sports did you participate in? _____

_____

Which subjects did you enjoy? _____

_____

Name a favorite teacher who inspired you and tell me why. _____

_____

_____

_____

Grandma, share a story about learning to do something new. _____

_____

_____

_____

_____

The truest greatness
lies in being kind,
the truest wisdom
in a happy mind.

ELLA WHEELER WILCOX

Loveliness needs not the foreign aid of ornament,
but is when unadorned adorned the most.

·

JAMES THOMSON

What clothing trends or hairstyles did you like or dislike when growing up?

_____

_____

_____

What sayings were popular when you were young? _____

_____

_____

_____

What was the style of the music during your teen years? What kind do you love now?

_____

_____

_____

How else did you and your peers express your individual styles? _____

_____

_____

_____

We are shaped and fashioned
by what we love.

JOHANN WOLFGANG VON GOETHE

_____

_____

A Girl's Dreams

Youth is the opportunity to do something and to become somebody.

THEODORE T. MUNGER

Did you wish for something special for a particular birthday? Did you get it? _____

_____

_____

What did you want to be when you grew up? _____

_____

_____

_____

_____

Which of your dreams have come true? _____

_____

_____

_____

> The world is a dream within a dream. As we grow older, each step is an awakening. The youth awakes as he thinks, from childhood.
>
> SIR WALTER SCOTT

What is your big dream for me, Grandmother? _____

_____

_____

_____

_____

Stories and Scenes

The joys I have possessed are ever mine;
Out of thy reach; behind eternity;
Hid in the sacred treasure of the past:
But blest remembrance brings them hourly back.

JOHN DRYDEN

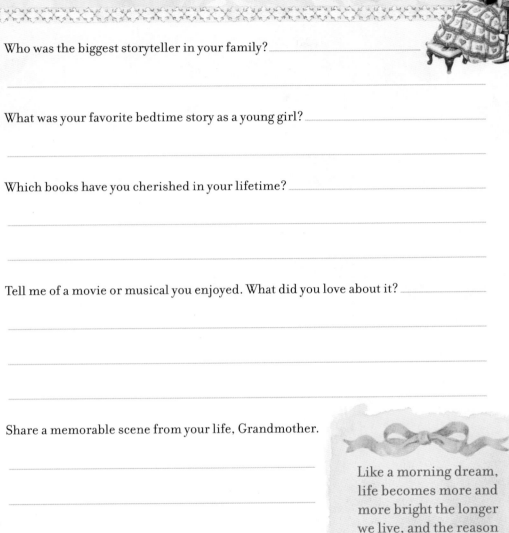

Who was the biggest storyteller in your family? _____

_____

What was your favorite bedtime story as a young girl? _____

_____

Which books have you cherished in your lifetime? _____

_____

_____

Tell me of a movie or musical you enjoyed. What did you love about it? _____

_____

_____

_____

Share a memorable scene from your life, Grandmother.

_____

_____

_____

_____

_____

_____

Like a morning dream, life becomes more and more bright the longer we live, and the reason of everything appears more clear. What has puzzled us before seems less mysterious, and the crooked paths look straighter as we approach the end.

JEAN PAUL RICHTER

17

The Beauty of Creation

As dew to the blossom, and bud to the bee, as the
scent to the rose, are those memories to me.

AMELIA B. WELBY

What did you love to do outside as a child? _____

_____

_____

What is your favorite flower or tree? _____

_____

_____

Where would you choose to go if you could visit any scenic area in the world? ____

_____

_____

Share with me a few of the joys of nature you hope I discover. _____

_____

_____

_____

Nature is beautiful, always beautiful! Every little flake of snow is a perfect crystal, and they fall together as gracefully as if fairies of the air caught water-drops and made them into artificial flowers to garland the wings of the wind!

LYDIA M. CHILD

19

Adventure Tales

Children and genius have
the same master organ in
common—inquisitiveness.
Let childhood have its way,
and as it began where genius
begins, it may find what
genius finds.

EDWARD BULWER-LYTTON

Describe an adventure you had as a kid.

_____

_____

What adventure do you still want to enjoy?

_____

_____

If you could take me on one great adventure, what would it be?

_____

_____

_____

Share a memory about a journey or experience that impacted your life.

_____

_____

Curiosity is as
much the parent of
attention, as attention
is of memory.

RICHARD WHATELY

21

Friends

Of all the things which wisdom provides to make life entirely
happy, much the greatest is the possession of friendship.

EPICURUS

Who was your best friend during your school years? _____

_____

Who are your dear friends now? _____

_____

_____

What qualities do you think make the best kind of friend? _____

_____

_____

_____

Did you have a favorite pet (a special furry friend) while growing up? _____

_____

_____

Share a story or memory about you and a friend. _____

_____

_____

_____

Stay is a charming word in a friend's vocabulary.

AMOS BRONSON ALCOTT

Stories from Hearth and Home

Every house where
Love abides,
And friendship is a guest,
Is surely home, and home, sweet home:
For there the heart can rest.

HENRY VAN DYKE

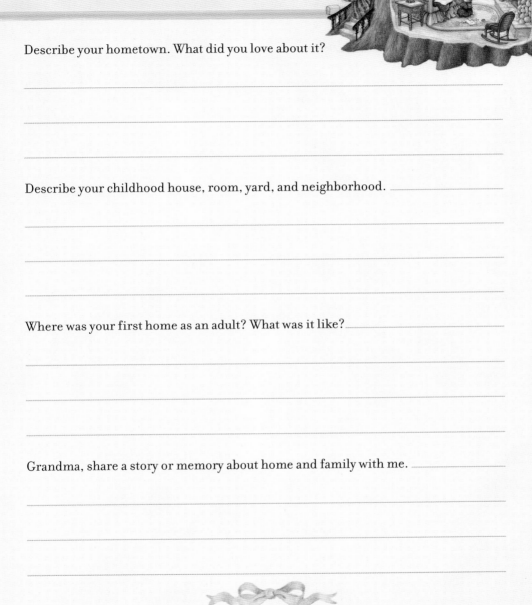

Describe your hometown. What did you love about it?

_____

_____

_____

Describe your childhood house, room, yard, and neighborhood. _____

_____

_____

_____

Where was your first home as an adult? What was it like?_____

_____

_____

_____

Grandma, share a story or memory about home and family with me. _____

_____

_____

_____

Blessed be the hand that prepares a pleasure for a child, for
there is no saying when and where it may again bloom forth.

DOUGLAS JERROLD

The Sound of Laughter

The laughter of girls is,
and ever was, among the
delightful sounds of earth.

THOMAS DE QUINCEY

What games did you play as a child?

_____

_____

_____

Come, my little children, here are songs for you;
Some are short and some are long, and all, all are new.
You must learn to sing them very small and clear,
Very true to time and tune and pleasing to the ear.

Mark the note that rises, mark the notes that fall.
Mark the time when broken, and the swing of it all.
So when night is come and you have gone to bed,
All the songs you love to sing shall echo in your head.

ROBERT LOUIS STEVENSON

What songs did you sing? _____

_____

Which games did you most enjoy playing with your kids? _____

_____

_____

What makes you laugh? Who makes you laugh? _____

_____

_____

_____

Which season of life has been the most fun? Why? _____

_____

_____

_____

_____

Table Talk

A hundred men
may make an
encampment, but
it takes a woman to
make a home.

CHINESE PROVERB

Home is the resort of love, of joy, of peace and plenty, where, supporting and supported, polished friends and dearest relatives mingle into bliss.

JAMES THOMSON

When you were young, what did your family talk about at the dinner table?

What was a typical breakfast for you?

When you were raising your family, what did you love about dinnertime?

What is a recipe or meal plan you'd love to pass along to your family?

Share a mealtime prayer or tradition you had as a child or as an adult.

Celebration Stories

A good laugh is sunshine in a house.

WILLIAM MAKEPEACE THACKERAY

What the best and wisest parent wants for his own child, that must the community want for all its children.

•

JOHN DEWEY

How did your family honor the holidays? _____
_____
_____
_____

What is a family holiday or birthday tradition you'd like future generations to know

and enjoy? _____
_____
_____
_____

Share one of your favorite celebration memories. _____
_____
_____
_____
_____
_____
_____

The cheerful live longest in years, and afterwards in our regards. Cheerfulness is the off-shoot of goodness.

CHRISTIAN NESTELL BOVEE

Love Stories

LOVER'S
LANE

*There is only
one happiness
in life, to love
and be loved.*

GEORGE SAND

Blessed is the influence of one true,
loving human soul on another.

GEORGE ELIOT

When did you fall in love with Grandpa? _____

_____

How did Grandpa ask you to marry him? _____

_____

Where and when were you married? What was your wedding like? _____

_____

_____

Describe the most romantic gift you have ever received or given. _____

_____

_____

Tell me about Grandpa. _____

_____

_____

_____

For the LORD is good.
His unfailing love continues forever,
and his faithfulness continues to each generation.

•

THE BOOK OF PSALMS

33

Faith and Family

My soul blesses the Great Father every day, that he has gladdened the earth with little children.

MARY HOWITT

When home is ruled according to God's Word, angels might be asked to stay with us, and they would not find themselves out of their element.

CHARLES H. SPURGEON

What was your religion growing up? _____

_____

What gives you hope today? _____

_____

_____

What is your prayer for me, Grandma? _____

_____

_____

_____

_____

Share a story or memory about the importance of faith and family. _____

_____

_____

_____

_____

_____

_____

Memorable Moments

Our home joys are the most delightful earth affords, and the joy of parents in their children is the most holy joy of humanity.

JOHANN HEINRICH PESTALOZZI

Do you have a special memory of your grandparents and parents? _____

_____

_____

_____

What aspect of your family life gave you comfort as a girl? _____

_____

_____

_____

What did you enjoy doing with your mom? Your dad? _____

_____

_____

_____

Which world events were most influential in your life? _____

_____

Memory, the
daughter of
Attention, is the
teeming mother
of Wisdom.
•
MARTIN TUPPER

_____

_____

_____

New Chapters:

BECOMING A PARENT AND GRANDPARENT

It seems but to-day! Oh, how proud am I now
As I lay welcome kisses on baby's wee brow!
A Grandmother, I? How the bright years have flown
Since I was a child scarce to maidenhood grown!

•

MARY D. BRINE, FROM *GRANDMA'S MEMORIES*

*Grandchildren are the crowning glory of the aged;
parents are the pride of their children.*

•

THE BOOK OF PROVERBS

What was going on in your life and in the world when you found out you were pregnant?

_____

_____

List the names of your children. Are any of them named after relatives? _____

_____

_____

_____

What was going on in your life and in the world when you found out you were going to

be a grandparent? _____

_____

_____

_____

Share a story or your fondest memories so far of being a parent and a grandparent.

_____

_____

_____

_____

_____

Legacies

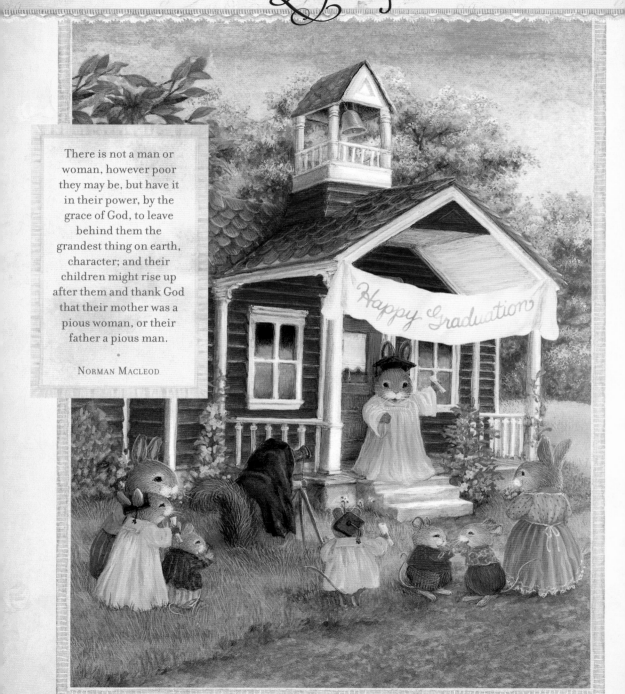

There is not a man or woman, however poor they may be, but have it in their power, by the grace of God, to leave behind them the grandest thing on earth, character; and their children might rise up after them and thank God that their mother was a pious woman, or their father a pious man.

Norman Macleod

Happy Graduation

Describe a person who greatly influenced your life. What did you learn from them?

_____

_____

_____

_____

What strong traits are part of our family's legacy?

_____

_____

_____

What family stories have been passed down to you?

_____

_____

_____

_____

_____

_____

> *Don't judge each day by the harvest you reap, but by the seeds you plant.*
>
> ROBERT LOUIS STEVENSON

Your Ongoing Story

God sends children for another purpose than merely to keep up the race—to enlarge our hearts, to make us unselfish, and full of kindly sympathies and affections; to give our souls higher aims, to call out all our faculties to extended enterprise and exertion; and to bring round our fire-side bright faces and happy smiles, and loving tender hearts.

MARY HOWITT

What do you love about this time of life? _____

_____

_____

If you were going to give your life story a title, what would it be? _____

_____

What would this chapter be called? _____

_____

Share a story or memory that illuminates something about yourself, Grandmother.

_____

_____

_____

_____

_____

_____

Those who loved you and were helped by you will
remember you when forget-me-nots have withered.
Carve your name on hearts, not on marble.

CHARLES H. SPURGEON

No matter what you've done for yourself or for humanity, if you can't look back on having given love and attention to your own family, what have you really accomplished?

ELBERT HUBBARD

What do you want me to know about your personal story, Grandma?

What is your heart message for me?

Dear _____

_____

_____

_____

_____

_____

_____

_____

_____

_____

_____

_____

You will find as you look back upon your life that the
moments that stand out above everything else are the
moments when you have done things in the spirit of love.

HENRY DRUMMOND

Women are the books,
the arts, the academes,
that show, contain and
nourish all the world.

SHAKESPEARE

This memory book is created by

_____

with great love for

_____

This is my story, this is my song...

Frances Crosby, "Blessed Assurance"